MAISIE PARRISH is a se...
artist. She started her ...
'Maisie Doughs', five ...
being inspired by a ve...
basket on the kitchen w...
house. Since then Maisie has worked
many eighteen-hour days developing her
successful craft business.

Maisie Dough models are now sold at
home and abroad. Now, in this
Workstation, Maisie shares the methods
and techniques which make her models
so appealing to people worldwide.

Dough Craft

WORKSTATION

WORKSTATION is a new concept comprising all
the elements you need to start
the art of Doughcraft.

The first 48 pages are an introduction to this
fascinating craft with clear, full colour illustrations
including many step-by-step doughcraft models to
make. The last eight pages provide templates
to enable you to make the charming models
featured in the book.

MAISIE PARRISH

A DESIGN EYE BOOK

First published in 1995 by Design Eye Ltd.
The Corn Exchange, Market Square,
Bishops Stortford HERTS CM23 3XF

© 1995 Design Eye Holdings Ltd.

ISBN 1 872700 38 1

The Design Eye Team

Michael Tout
Lee Robinson
Aline Serra Littlejohn
Sally Symes
Joanne Coles

With thanks to our contributors
Rita Wüthrich, Millions Design,
Paula Soper and Pamela Hopkinson.
Photography by Chris Linton.

Manufactured in China.

CONTENTS

INTRODUCTION

Congratulations - you have taken the first step towards beginning a craft that I know will bring you tremendous satisfaction. From very simple ingredients and tools - most of which are probably already in your kitchen - you can create something very special of your own. I hope that, by the time you have mastered the final projects, you will be hooked for life.

Working with dough is very therapeutic as well as creative. It can turn what could otherwise be a boring day into something so pleasurable that if you're not careful doughcraft could take up most of your time. Doughcraft is definitely addictive!

However, creating something from a lump of raw material is not always as easy as one might think. It takes practice, patience and, above all, perseverance. The many projects in this book have been carefully chosen so that you can begin with small simple things,

like brooches and fridge magnets, and build up to much more elaborate models like a bowl of fruit and flowers or a thatched cottage. Each project is broken down into step-by-step stages with clear instructions, so that even if you have never tried any modelling before, you can begin right away making your own attractive decorations.

This Workstation includes some of the basic equipment that you need to get started right away. The best place to work is in the comfort of your own kitchen where you will find that most of the other items you need are already at hand.

The paints supplied with the Workstation are water based and you can mix them together to increase your colour range.

Leave all your inhibitions behind, and master the basic techniques - you will apply these to everything you make and soon you will be able to design and make your own dough models for family and friends.

MATERIALS AND TECHNIQUES

If you have a little flour in your kitchen, then you can start doughcraft right away. With water, salt and a little oil and the help of ordinary kitchen utensils, as well as the tools and paints supplied with this Workstation - you are all set to begin.

TOOLS AND UTENSILS

Ideally all tools and utensils should be made from wood, plastic or stainless steel. The salt in the dough corrodes tin and prevents the tool or cutter from making a clean cut.

Improvisation is the key - items which would otherwise be thrown away can prove to be your most innovative tools. Listed below are some important basic items. You will probably have most of them in your home already.

You will be able to find lots of things in your kitchen to make patterns on your dough. You can improvise cutters with lids from coffee jars or use a wine glass. Good tools are expensive and you can add these to your workbox as you progress.

A glass worktop saver is an ideal working surface, but it is not essential. When you are modelling the dough work on a sheet of greaseproof paper. You can cover the baking sheet with greaseproof paper and work directly onto it. The dough is baked at relatively low temperatures, so you can also work and bake the dough on a

small hardwood board. Cover the board first with greaseproof paper. If you are baking at the lowest temperatures, used for coloured dough, then you may also cover the baking sheet or board with plastic food wrap, but remember this plastic film will melt on higher temperatures.

1. Rolling pin: a small one, made of wood or nylon, is more useful than a full size rolling pin.

2. Sharp knife with a smooth, unserrated edge

3. Scissors

4. Pizza cutter

5. Set of round pastry cutters in graduated sizes, made of plastic or nylon

6. Baking sheet, at least one. You will probably want to acquire more as you begin to make more and more models.

7. Greaseproof paper for working on and for covering the baking sheet.

8. Plastic food wrap

9. Garlic crusher

10. Modelling tools supplied with your Workstation. The serrated-edge tool is useful for making 'stitching' marks on Teddy Bears and other toys, while the rounded end is for modelling

shapes like ears. The other tool has a cutting edge with a scooped shape at the other end for creating a smile.

11. Water soluble paints are supplied with the Workstation, mix the paints in the palettes provided to increase your range of colours.

12. Paintbrush, remember the pointed end of the paintbrush is a useful modelling tool too.

13. Cocktail sticks are very useful for fine work when a delicate point is called for.

14. A clean soapy cloth and a towel are essential to keep the salt from building up on your hands while you are working.

15. A plastic box, for example, an ice cream container makes an ideal place to keep all your bits and pieces.

TECHNIQUES

The techniques and methods of working used in this Workstation are the ones I use and feel most comfortable with. As you become more experienced and at ease with the craft, you will find your own ways of working, this is fine, use the methods you prefer.

THE DOUGH

The recipe I prefer is given below. The correct proportions should be carefully measured out. Too much of one thing and not enough of another will affect the outcome. This recipe will make enough dough for you to make several items.

You will need:
◆ 2 level cups of plain flour
◆ 1 level cup of cooking salt
◆ ¾ cup of lukewarm water
◆ ½ teaspoon of cooking oil
  (optional)
◆ Mixing bowl
◆ Wooden spoon
◆ Measuring jug
◆ Plastic bag

To make the dough:
1. Blend the flour and salt together in a mixing bowl.
2. Pour on the water and oil.
3. Stir well with a wooden spoon then press together to form a ball with your hands as you would when making pastry.
4. Remove the dough and place it on the worksurface. Knead firmly with the ball of your hand as you would if you were making bread.
5. Continue to knead for about 10 minutes until all the ingredients are well-blended and the dough feels smooth and supple. Working the dough well at this stage will give the best results.

TESTING THE DOUGH

Make a long sausage shape and hold it up for a few seconds. If the dough does not stretch it is good - if it does stretch, then it is too wet and more flour must be added until you have a firm consistency.

Flour varies a great deal and so the amount of water you need to add to your dough will also vary, more or less depending upon the flour, but you will be able to judge this with a little practice.

Dough that is too wet is the usual problem, but dough can also be too dry after kneading. If so, just add a little oil to the palm of your hand and continue to knead, the dough will become supple and smooth.

When you are satisfied that your dough is the right consistency, leave it to rest for up to one hour, wrapped in an airtight plastic bag. This will prevent the air getting to it and drying it out. Any dough that you are not using should be kept in this way.

Unused dough will keep for up to two days. After this time it will become sticky and wet. For best results throw away old dough and begin again with a fresh mix.

COLOURING THE DOUGH

At this stage it is possible to divide up the dough into portions and colour each one using a vegetable food colour. These colours are available in liquid or paste form, either can be used in the following way.

Take a small portion of dough and moisten the surface with a little water. Smooth the food colouring over the dough with your finger, this will help the colour to develop. Knead the colour into the dough, adding more if necessary to achieve the desired shade.

Repeat this process for each colour, keeping each portion of dough in a separate bag until required.

For the purpose of demonstration in the step-by-step instructions this is the method I have used as it does give a more professional look to the finished product, and shows each stage of the modelling more clearly.

Vegetable food colouring is safe to use with children but it can stain quite badly. Wear clothes that you do not mind soiling.

Remember also that coloured dough should not be cooked at temperatures greater than 100°C (230°F).

PAINTING DOUGH

Watercolours
Four watercolours are provided with this Workstation. You can mix them to make many more colours. Take care when painting not to

saturate the dough with too much water on your brush.

For strong colours use less water and apply two coats of paint, leaving them to dry in between.

For pastel shades, mix the paint with more water, you can produce a pleasing effect by letting each colour flow over into another shade.

When you have used up the paints supplied with the Workstation, any good quality watercolour paints can be used. Watercolours are best used when working with children as they wash out easily if spilled onto clothing.

Acrylics

Acrylic paints are very quick and simple to use because they cover well and dry quickly, allowing another colour or pattern to be painted on top within 15 minutes.

Do protect your clothing as acrylics dry hard and are permanent. They should be washed out at once if they get onto clothes or kitchen surfaces.

Drawing on doughs

Details and facial features can be painted onto the dough with a fine brush - the black paint supplied with the Workstation is useful for this. You may also find a permanent felt-tip pen is very useful for this purpose. These come in a wide variety of colours and thicknesses. I find it is easier to draw on a dough that has been varnished otherwise the tip of the pen will soon wear away and the lines are not smooth.

Colour blends

Painting is very enjoyable and you can experiment with colour to create your own special touches. Adding white to your colours will make them lighter, black darker. The addition of white to your colour range will be very useful.

Red + Blue = Purple
Red + White = Pink
Yellow + Blue = Green
Green + Red = Brown
Black + White = Grey

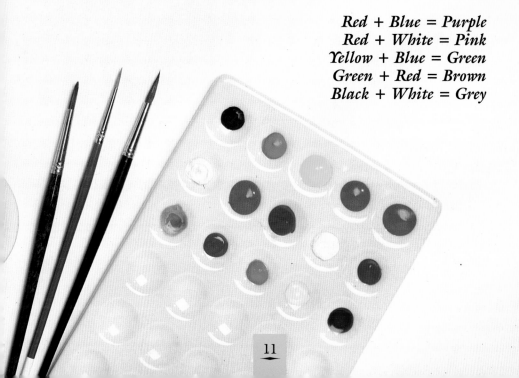

FIXING PARTS TOGETHER

This part of the operation is very important. Wet your paintbrush in clean water, brush it over the parts to be joined and push them together. You will find the plastic tools useful to help press the dough surfaces together. Join pieces before baking. Every part of a dough model is fixed together in this way.

BAKING THE DOUGH

A fan assisted oven is my preference, as the temperature is the same throughout the oven. Remember if your oven does not have a fan, that temperatures will be higher in the top of the oven than the bottom. However, all ovens vary and you may have to adjust the temperatures should you find them too high for your own oven. Temperatures are given in both centigrade and fahrenheit.

METHOD 1
Required for coloured doughs
This method dries out the doughs in 12 to 36 hours depending on their size and thickness. This is the most successful method and the more expensive one. The lower temperature helps prevent colours from fading. Start from a cold oven 75°- 180°C (165°- 350°F), fan assisted 50°C (120°F).

METHOD 2
Ideal for natural doughs
Start from a cold oven 75°- 90°C (165°- 190°F) for two hours then gradually increase the temperature every two hours until you reach 125°C (260°F).

METHOD 3
Suitable for smaller items
Bake for two to three hours at 110°-120°C (230°-250°F).
    You may find it helpful to keep the oven door open for the first few minutes in order for the surface of the dough to dry out evenly, especially for coloured dough.
    Once the dough has cooked enough to allow you to remove it from the baking sheet, place it on an oven rack to enable the air to circulate freely around it.
    Should you wish to bake dried flowers with the dough do not exceed temperatures of 50°C (120°F).

IS THE DOUGH COOKED?

Test your dough by tapping it on the back. Uncooked dough will sound dull when tapped with your nail but a cooked piece will have a hollow ring.

VARNISHING

Whichever method of painting or colouring your dough you have chosen, the finished piece must also be varnished to help keep out the moisture. The varnish must completely cover every part of the dough, take care not to miss any crevice otherwise the moisture in the air will be absorbed and the dough will soften.

Choosing a varnish for the first time can be bewildering as there are so many to choose from. I suggest that you go for a clear polyurethane matt or gloss solvent-based varnish. A water-based varnish will cause a chemical reaction in the dough and it will crumble as a result. Always apply varnish in a well-ventilated room and clean brushes in the appropriate solvent thoroughly after use.

To varnish the dough:
Use a dry clean brush and apply varnish all over the dough. Leave to dry for 12 hours then give a second coat. The more your dough is to be exposed to temperature changes the more coats it will need.

WARNING:
this operation should not be attempted by children because of the solvent in the varnish.

Dough figures are *hydroscopic*, by their very nature they are likely to attract moisture. Dough figures should be kept dry at all times. Do not hang them near outside doors or open windows. Hang them on inside rather than outside walls as they are usually warm during cold weather.

Should you find that your dough has been in the wrong place and it has begun to soften, place it in a warm place such as an airing cupboard until it has become hard again. It may need to be revarnished to seal it, but it will then be as good as new.

BROOCHES AND FRIDGE MAGNETS

These projects are ideal for the complete beginner. You can make an assortment of these small items and bake them together on one baking sheet. At the same time, fridge magnets and brooches make very attractive gifts for your family and friends, and they are ideal projects for children to join in making.

Once you have tried your hand at the basic techniques introduced with these small projects, you can go on to create your own designs.

Magnets and brooch pins are supplied with this Workstation. When you have used these up, you can buy more from any good craft shop. The magnet or pin should be glued to the back of the model after the coats of varnish have dried hard. Clear adhesive or a two-part epoxy resin glue are both suitable.

You will need:

- ◆ The basic utensils listed on page 6
- ◆ A quantity of basic dough
- ◆ Magnets
- ◆ Brooch fixings
- ◆ Adhesive
- ◆ Cocktail stick or similar fine tool

FLOWER BROOCH
For the base:
Roll out the dough to ½ cm (¼ in) thickness. Cut out a round shape approximately 2cm (¾ in) in diameter.

To make leaves:
1. Roll a small ball of dough into a pear shape and flatten it between finger and thumb.
2. Make leaf markings with a knife or other tool. Make 5 larger leaves and 3 smaller ones.
3. Place the 5 larger leaves around the base of the circle and then position the smaller ones between.

HAT MAGNET
To make the hat:
1. Roll out the dough to ½ cm (¼ in) thickness.
2. Using a round cutter or upturned wine glass, cut out a small round shape 5cm (2¼ in) in diameter. Smooth the edges to soften with your fingers.
3. Make stitch marks around the brim with the cocktail stick or other tool.
4. Place a small round of dough in the centre of the circle for the crown of the hat. Press down slightly to flatten.

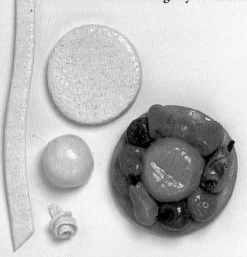

To make the flower:
1. Make another 5 very small leaf shapes for the petals and place these in a circle on your worktop so that they are joined.
2. Slide a knife under the circle of petals and place them over the leaves on the base.
3. Place a small ball of dough in the centre and arrange the petals to look like a flower.
4. Prick the flower centre with the cocktail stick to give it texture.

To make the ribbon:
1. Roll out the dough making it ¼ cm (⅛ in) thick.
2. Using a knife or pizza wheel, cut a strip 14cm (5¾ in) long and ½cm (¼ in) wide to make a ribbon.
3. Place the ribbon around the crown of the hat, leaving tails. Trim to size if the ribbon is too long. When the length is right, fix it to the hat.
4. Make a bow from the ribbon trimmings and fix it to the hat.

TEDDY BEAR MAGNET

To make the body:

Make a small oval shape, its size will determine the finished size of the bear. These instructions can be followed to make any size of Teddy Bear.

To make the legs:

1. Roll a cigar shape with your fingers.
2. Lay the cigar shape in front of you on your worktop and with one hand, push one rounded end backwards to form the foot. Repeat this for the end.
3. This will take a little practice to perfect, so keep on trying until the shape is correct. When you are satisfied that you have it right, cut into two halves. You now have two legs with a foot on each.
4. Make a diagonal cut across the top of the leg so that it fits the bear's body perfectly.
5. Fix one leg to each side of the body at the hip joint.

To make the head:

1. Roll a small round of dough into a pear shape. Push up the point to make a nose and flatten slightly. Push up to form the snout.
2. Make hole in the snout with the end of a paint brush and insert a piece of pear-shaped dough for nose.
3. Using a cocktail stick, make stitch marks from the top of the head to the base of the snout.
4. Fix the head to the body.

To make the ears:

1. Place two small rounds of dough should be on either side of the head. As it is so small, use the end of a paint brush to help secure each ear.

To make the bow:

1. Roll out a narrow strip and cut two ends diagonally for tails.
2. Roll a second strip, fold each end into the middle.
3. Turn the bow over, squeeze the centre, use a modelling tool to shape knot. Attach the tails.

To make the arms:

1. Make another cigar shape rounded at both ends as before. Cut it in half and you now have two arms. The paws are the rounded ends. If you have made them too long trim them now to the desired length.
2. Make a diagonal cut across the top of each arm and fix to the shoulders.

5. Make eyes on either side of the head with the cocktail stick.

To make the hat:

1. Roll out a piece of dough to ½cm (¼in) thickness and cut out a round 2cm (¾in) in diameter. Cut straight along the back making a half moon shape, and place it on the head.
2. Cut a length of dough for the ribbon and cross it under the beak.
3. Fix a bow on the ribbon.

DUCK BROOCH

To make the body:

Make a small round of dough into a pear shape, lay it on the board and push the tail end gently upwards.

To make the wing:

1. Do exactly the same thing again only with a very small piece of dough.
2. Place the wing on to body and make feather marks with tool or knife.

To make the neck and head:

1. Roll out a piece of dough to a cigar shape ½cm (¼in) thick with your fingers. Gently bring forward one rounded end with your finger to form the head.
2. Trim the bottom end off to a diagonal shape to fit the body and fix into place. Arrange the neck and head into the required position.
3. With the end of a paintbrush, push a hole into the end of the head where the beak is to be placed.
4. Roll out dough between the fingers and shape for the beak. Place it into hole. Put in two nostrils with a cocktail stick.

To make the legs and feet:

1. Roll out dough into a cigar shape. Cut off enough for a small leg, flatten a round of dough into shape for a foot. Mark the webbed feet with a tool or knife.

BACON & EGGS MAGNET

As you can see from the illustration, the whole plate comes to life once you have painted everything.

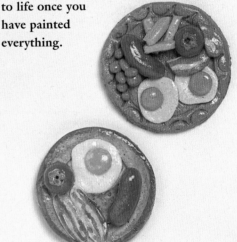

1. For the plate, cut out a round shape with a small wine glass or cutter.
2. For the egg whites, squeeze small piece of dough between your fingers to make it into an irregular shape.
3. For the yolk, place a small round of dough just off-centre on the egg white.
4. Roll and model sausage shapes, beans, tomatoes and chips with your fingers.
5. For the bacon rashers, work a small sausage into a flat irregular shape with your fingers.

CARROT MAGNETS

1. Make three pear shapes of dough and elongate each one slightly by rolling the end on your worktop to form a carrot shape.
2. With the back of a knife, mark the upper surface of each carrot from end to end.
3. To make carrot tops, fill the garlic press with dough and squeeze it out. Arrange these as desired.

PIG BROOCH

To make the body, legs and tail:

1. Roll a small ball of dough into a pear shape for the body. The size of the body will determine the size of the finished pig. Make it smaller or larger at this point.
2. Roll out a length of dough and cut two legs. Make a diagonal cut at top of each to fit body.
3. Attach to the body.
4. With the back of a knife, make a line along the body to where the tail will be attached.
5. Roll very thin piece of dough and fix it at the back in a curl.

To make the head:

1. Roll a small round of dough into a pear shape. Push up the point to make a nose and flatten slightly.
2. Fix the head to the body, turning the face of the pig so that it is looking at you.

To make the ears:

1. Shape two very small cigar shapes for the ears. Cut to size if they are too long at one end, leaving a point for the end of the ear.
2. Fix them to the side of the head and arrange them to suit.

CAKE MAGNET

1. Roll out a piece of dough to 1cm (½ in) thickness. Cut out three rounds with a cutter or upturned wine glass.
2. Roll out the dough very thinly and make three more rounds of the same size for the filling.
3. Place these rounds alternately one on top of the other until you have a complete cake.
4. Roll some dough into two lengths and twist them together for the decoration on the top of the cake.
5. Finish off with cherries.

To make a big slice

1. Take a sharp knife and cut out a very large slice. This will make an ideal brooch or magnet. You have the remaining cake for another magnet.

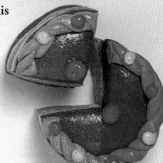

ALPHABET BEAR

T his is a gift that you really can personalise for yourself or a friend. It is perfect for Valentine's Day, or any special occasion. You can make the letter match an initial or even spell out a full name i.e. L U C Y. Use bright colours for older children or perhaps pink or blue for a new baby.

A complete alphabet to copy is in the back of the book.

You will need:
◆ The basic utensils listed on page 6
◆ A quantity of basic dough
◆ Length of string

To make the letters:
The instructions are given for a letter 'b'. Make one for practice, and you will soon see how you can form any other letter of the alphabet.

1. Make three strips of dough by rolling them out with your fingers like a pencil until they are 50cm (20in) long. This length should be enough to make any letter.
2. Pinch the three ends together at the top, leaving the bottom ends free.
3. Roll them together into a twist like a stick of Barley Sugar to a finished length of approximately 40cm (16in). Pinch bottom ends together, this helps to keep them in place.
4. Measure 15cm (6in) and cut off, leaving the other piece of 25cm (10in). The short piece makes the vertical strip.
5. Place one end of the 25cm (10in) strip half way down the vertical piece and curve round to join at the bottom of the letter. You may have to cut off

any excess at this point. Make sure that all joins are pushed firmly together. Now you have a perfect letter 'b'.

To make the hanging loop:
1. Roll a small ball of dough in your palms and then squeeze it between finger and thumb to about 2cm (¾in) diameter.
2. Cut the string to 5cm (2¼in). Wet both ends and press them into the disc of dough.
3. Slide the disc underneath the letter and press it so that the ends of the string are firmly sandwiched between the letter and the disc of dough, leaving the loop free.

To make the body:

1. Roll out dough into an oval shape in your hands 4cm (1½in) long. This should look like an egg, place it on the curve of the letter.

2. With a smaller piece of dough make another egg shape, but this time roll it out into a cigar shape so that it has rounded ends to a length of 10cm x 1cm (4in x ½in). This will make two legs with the feet.

3. Make each foot by pushing the ends of the dough backwards. Cut in the middle to separate. Now you have two legs with feet.

4. Make a diagonal cut at the top of each leg to fit the body. You will have to adjust the inside leg to suit the length required as it will be shorter than the outside leg. Fix the legs to the body.

5. Make the arms by rolling out a cigar shape to approximately 7cm x 1cm (2¾in x ½in), then cut it in half.

6. Make diagonal cut at the top of each arm to fit the body and adjust to the length required. Fix the arms to the shoulders.

To make the head:

1. Make a round of dough with your hand, smaller than the body, and mould it into a pear shape.

2. Push the narrow end backwards to form a snout, you may need to practise this. Place it into position, fixing it firmly to the body and the letter.

3. Make a tiny pear shape for the tip of the nose. Press the end of a paintbrush into the tip of the snout and fix a black nose into the hole.

4. Make nostrils with a cocktail stick.

5. With a cocktail stick or fine pointed tool make stitch marks from the top of the head to the end of the nose. Place an eye hole on either side of the stitching, equal distances apart.

6. Make three more stitch marks under the nose to the mouth using the end of the brush make a hole for the mouth.

7. Roll two small balls of dough and squeeze slightly into shape for the ears. Place the ears evenly on each side of the head, fixing firmly into place with the end of a paintbrush .

7. Tuck the bear into the curve of the letter as shown. You will have to experiment with each different letter of the alphabet, arranging the arms and legs until the model looks right.

To make the bow:

1. Roll out a small piece of dough to
¼ cm (⅛ in) thickness.
2. Using a knife or pizza wheel, cut
out a length for tails 3cm (1¼ in) long
by 1cm (½ in) wide.
3. Cut another length for the bow
5cm (2¼ in) long by 1½ cm (¾ in) wide.
4. Cut the length for the tails in half
and place side by side, make a
diagonal cut at both ends. Place under
chin of the Teddy.
5. To make the bow, turn both ends of
the dough into the middle to meet
each other. Turn face down and pinch
together with your fingers in the
middle.
6. Place under chin of the Teddy,
covering the top of the tails, and make
two marks with a tool or back of a
knife to form the finished bow.

To finish:

1. Finish off the feet with small
rounds of black dough to make paws.
2. Cut three lengths of string 12cm
(5in) long, fixing them to the
Teddy's paw and cover with a small
pad of dough to fix. Place the
other ends to the top of the letter.
3. To make the hearts, roll a
round of dough in your palm
into a pear shape, press down
slightly to flatten. With a tool
or the back of a knife, make a
mark in the top to form a heart
shape. Make three hearts and
fix them over the ends of the
string.

PENGUIN

This comical little character will gladden any heart. There are many ways you can adapt the basic body shape: make a lady penguin by putting on a bonnet with a bow under the chin; alter the position of the flippers upwards or in front of the body. For Christmas, add a festive red and green bobble hat and striped scarf; for anniversaries or other special occasions he looks very dignified with a top hat.

Make and collect as many penguin characters as you can dream up - enjoy yourself!

You will need:
◆ The utensils listed on page 6
◆ A quantity of basic dough

To make the head:

1. Roll a round of dough big enough for the head. Try it against the body first before fixing to ensure it is the correct proportion to the body, then fix.
2. Flatten the face slightly.
3. Using a cocktail stick or tool make stitch marks from the top of the head to the centre of the face. Press a dent into the head where the beak is to be positioned.
4. For the eyes, make two oval shapes for the whites and place them evenly on each side of the stitchmarks. Put in black lines for the eyes.
5. For the cheeks, make an oblong shape. Roll it between your fingers to make it narrow in the middle, keeping each end the same thickness.
6. Make the beak in the shape of a carrot and place it where you have made the dent, in the hole over the cheeks. Fix firmly. Mark the beak at the sides using a knife.
7. Make a bow with tails, as for the Alphabet Bear.
8. Flatten two ovals for the feet, mark and fix to the body.

To make the body:

1. Make a round shape of dough in your hand and roll out to a pear shape. This will be the body. Lay it on a board or tray and flatten slightly. Make a small cut at the base to form the legs.
2. For the flippers, roll out a cigar shape to approximately 8 cm (3¼ in) long and cut in half. Flatten gently between your fingers.
3. Place the straight edge at the shoulder and secure, turning up the rounded end to form the flipper.
4. For the chest, cut out a small thin oval, place under the chin and make stitch marks down the middle.

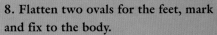

TEDDY BEARS

Everyone loves a Teddy Bear and here are four lovely designs to add to any collection, or give with love. Make a basic Teddy Bear and dress it up as a boy or girl, add decorations and accessories - it's so easy and a lot of fun dressing them.

Make the basic Teddy following the instructions for the Alphabet Bear on page 20.

TEDDY WITH FLOWERS

Add a bow, with tails, following the instructions given for the Alphabet Bear on page 20.

Use a garlic press to make stems for the flowers and fix them to the paw. Then arrange colourful flowers around the paw.

TEDDY WITH BOOK

For the book, cut a strip of red dough 5cm x 2cm (2in x ¾in) for the cover, then a strip 4½ cm x 2cm (1¾in x ¾in) in white for pages.

Moisten the red dough with a brush and place the white dough on top. Fold in half to make a book. Mark the spine with a knife and place the finished book under Teddy's arm.

TEDDY WITH PRESENT

Make small oblong of dough for the present. Cut thin strips of dough and place them across and down for the ribbon. Finish with a small flower. Place it under Teddy's arm.

SAILOR TEDDY

To make the collar:

1. Roll out dough 1cm x 5cm x ½cm thick (½ in x 2in x ¼ in).
2. Cut a diagonal line in the middle to separate, and joint the diagonal ends into a V-shape.
3. Place the collar on to the Teddy. Cut out a very thin strip to edge with a contrast colour and place it on top of the collar.
4. Finish off with a small tie.

To make the hat:

1. Place small round of dough on top of Teddy's head.
2. Cut a small thin ribbon to go all the way around the hat. Make a small V-cut to finish.

CLOWN

Clowns are a big favourite, and this little character will bring a smile to everyone's face. This model is very simple to make, with a basic body shape that can be used for many things. You can try many variations in colours and dress details which will make each clown look quite individual and different from the others. This model is a real opportunity to use lots of colour, make each clown as bright and outrageous as you like.

You will need:
◆ The basic utensils listed on page 6
◆ A quantity of basic dough
◆ String

To make the body:
1. Make a ball of dough into a pear shape - the basic shape for any clown.
2. Make a hanging loop from string and a disc of dough in the same way as for the Alphabet Bear on page 20, slide it under the body of the clown and secure firmly.

To make the trousers:
1. Roll out dough to ¼ cm (⅛ in) thickness and cut out following the template in the back of the book.

2. Place on the body, slightly below the waistline in a curve to make him look portly. Tuck in around the edges and trim.

3. Using the tip of your knife, make a small cut at the base of the body to give the effect of legs.

4. For the feet, shape two rounds of dough into pear shapes, and place in a comical turned out position .

To make the arms:

1. Roll a piece of dough into a cigar shape, about 1cm (½ in) thick and cut in half. Cut the top of each piece diagonally so it fits the shoulder. Attach to the body.

2. Roll two small balls of dough for the hands and fix them to the wrists.

To make braces:

1. Cut thin strips of dough following the template in the back of the book. Make a slit at one end.

2. Fix the braces from the shoulder, spreading the end open. Fix two buttons on each.

To make the head:

1. Roll a ball of dough. Hold it against the body to check that it is the correct proportion.

2. With the end of a paintbrush make a hole for the nose. Roll a small pear shape and fix it to the face.

3. For each eye, make a cross, drop a small spot of black dough in the centre.

4. For the ears, make two rounds the size of a pea.

5. Give the clown a big smile with the curved ended tool.

6. Make strands of hair with the garlic press, and place over each ear.

7. Finish off the clown with a big bow.

SNOWMAN WITH HAT AND SCARF

Make this jolly little snowman using the same body as the Alphabet Bear on page 20, repeating the same technique until you come to the head.

Doughcraft is such fun and the materials are so economical, you can make whole snowman families to give as gifts or as a decorative theme for a winter party. Or adapt the Alphabet Bear for Christmas presents and make Alphabet Snowmen instead!

You will need:

◆ The basic utensils listed on page 6
◆ A quantity of basic dough

To make the head:

1. Roll out a perfectly round ball in a suitable size for the body. Try it against the body to check that the proportions are correct.
2. Fix the head firmly to the body.
3. With the end of a paintbrush, make a hole in the centre of the head for the nose. The nose of course, is a small carrot. Roll it out, push into the hole and secure it.
4. Give the snowman a big smile using the end of the modelling tool.
5. Put black buttons down the front.

To make the hat:

1. Roll out dough to ¼ cm (⅛ in) thickness and cut out a round with an upturned wine glass. Place it on top of the snowman's head.
2. Make a small round of dough and press it on top of the hat brim, make a mark down the middle with a tool to secure it.

To make the scarf:

1. Cut two strips of dough in red and green approximately 2cm (¾ in) wide.
2. Use one colour for the scarf, and cut the other up to form the stripes. Place the stripes across the scarf.
3. Fringe one end.
4. Place the scarf around the neck with the fringed end hanging down.

SANTA CLAUS

Christmas comes but once a year and when it does you certainly need a Santa Claus. Make several of these to decorate your home with, he will also make an ideal gift.

Remember to wrap your dough Christmas decorations away very carefully after Christmas and keep them in a dry place. They will be as good as new the next year.

You will need:
- The basic utensils listed on page 6
- A quantity of basic dough
- A fork

To make Santa Claus

1. Make body in the same way as the clown (page 28) and attach the feet.
2. Cut a strip of dough for the belt, and fit it under the belly slightly to make him look more portly. Add a buckle and mark the details.
3. Make the arms and hands in the same way as for the clown.
4. Fix a hanging loop under the body.
5. Roll a piece of dough for the head. Attach it to the body.
6. Make a hole in middle of the face for the nose. Roll a small ball of dough for the nose and secure it in the hole.
7. Make 2 ears each the size of a pea and fix to the head.
8. Give Santa a big happy smile with the curved end of the tool.
9. Using a cocktail stick, make eyes.
10. Push some dough through the garlic press and twist very small strands for eyebrows and moustache.
11. For the beard, lay single strands of dough out on your worktop then, shape them into a crescent shape.
12. Slide a knife blade under the beard and place it on the face.

To make the hat:

1. Roll out dough to ¼ cm (⅛ in) thickness and cut out a large circle.
2. Arrange the circle across the front of the head and bring it to a point at one side. Do not attach point to side of head yet.
3. For the fur trimming, roll a strip of dough, use the fork to prick it all over.
4. Bring down the point of the hat and secure to side of head with a bobble.

CHRISTMAS CANDLE
HOLDERS

Every festive table needs to have a centrepiece. Both of these Christmas designs are sure to delight your family and guests. With the addition of an elegant candle - which could be red, green white, gold or silver - these models would make a lovely gift. Once you have made them both, perhaps you will be inspired to create your own designs.

You will need:
◆ The basic utensils listed on page 6
◆ A quantity of basic dough

SNOWMAN
To make the candleholder:
1. Cut out the template of the large star from the back of the book.
2. Roll out dough to 1cm (½in) thickness and place template on top, cutting around the shape with a knife.
3. Make ball of dough large enough to hold a candle. Place it centrally on top of the star, and with a candle, press into the middle to make a well. This well must be deep enough to hold the candle securely.

To make the leaves:
1. Make 5 large leaves and cover the points of the star. You will also need five smaller leaves which should be placed above but in line with the larger ones.
2. With the back of knife or tool mark the veins.

To make the snowman:
1. You will need 5 larger and 5 smaller balls of dough to make the body and head. Remember that the snowman is a very rounded shape which you will have to make flat on your worktop. Try to keep him rounded when fixing the parts together.
2. Fix small round to large round.
3. With the end of a paintbrush, make a small hole where the carrot nose will be fixed, and mark the eyes just above the nose on each side.
4. Put a smile on his face with the curved ended tool.

To make the hat and scarf:
1. Cut out a circle 2cm (¾in) in diameter. Place it on top of the head.
2. Use a ball of dough for the crown and press it down gently to secure.
3. Make the scarf by cutting thin strips of green dough and placing them on top of the red which is the background colour.

4. Place the scarf around the neck of the snowman and fringe the ends.

5. To position the snowmen, wet the base where they are to be placed and secure each one between the points of the star. Check that the size of the hole for the candle is correct before you begin baking the model.

POINSETTIA

Make a base with the star shape in red or green. Make five flowers following these instructions.

To make the leaves:

1. You will need to make 6 large leaves and 6 smaller ones. Mark veins on the 6 large leaves. Do not mark the smaller leaves.

2. Cut out a small round of dough approximately 2cm (¾ in) in diameter. The flower will be built up on this.

3. Arrange the larger leaves around it.

To make the flower:

1. Take the 6 small leaf shapes and lay them in a circle on your worktop. All 6 should be touching in a circle.

2. Slide the knife blade under the petals carefully and place them on top of the leaves.

3. Make a small ball of dough and drop it into the centre of the petals. Arrange the petals carefully round it.

4. Prick the centre of the flower with a cocktail stick to give it texture.

To fix the flowers to the base:

1. Before attaching the flowers to the base, make 5 small balls of dough approximately 2cm (¾ in) in diameter and place one between each point of the star. Flatten each one very slightly.

2. Very carefully slide a wet knife under each finished poinsettia and place it over the small round of dough.

CHRISTMAS DECORATIONS

Everyone will enjoy making decorations in time for Christmas. Even the smallest members of the family can join in with the simpler modelling and painting tasks, while you can assign yourself to doing the more difficult pieces. Make them in plain dough and paint them with your Workstation paints, or if you prefer, use coloured dough.

These decorations also make excellent Christmas presents, so start making them in good time. If you do not have festive pastry cutters, then use the templates provided at the back of this Workstation. Add flowers or bows, leaves or berries and make a whole batch which can be cooked on one baking tray.

You will need:
◆ The basic utensils listed on page 6
◆ A quantity of basic dough
◆ Glitter
◆ Glue
◆ Ribbon for hanging

1. Roll out a sheet of dough to ½ cm (¼ in) thick. Cut out the shapes using pastry cutters, or cut around the templates with the tip of a sharp straight-bladed knife.
2. Lift the shapes from the dough and soften edges with tool or your fingers to make them look more rounded.
3. To make larger shapes, use a thicker dough, cut out the shape then roll each one out to ½ cm (¼ in) thickness.
4. If you wish, make a pattern in the dough or around the edges with a fork or tool, or leave plain.
5. Make a hole for hanging in the top of each one by twisting the end of your paintbrush through to the other side. Then cook and varnish.

Painting the decorations:
If you use a natural coloured dough, you can use the paints provided with your Workstation to paint patterns on the shapes. Gold and silver poster paint can be bought from artists' and hobby shops.
To add glitter, spread a little glue where you wish to place the glitter. Lay the dough on a sheet of paper to catch the excess glitter and sprinkle it over the dough pieces.
Finish off with with pretty ribbon or glittery thread to hang the decorations.
The larger pieces are too heavy for a Christmas tree, hang them on a door or over a mantelpiece.

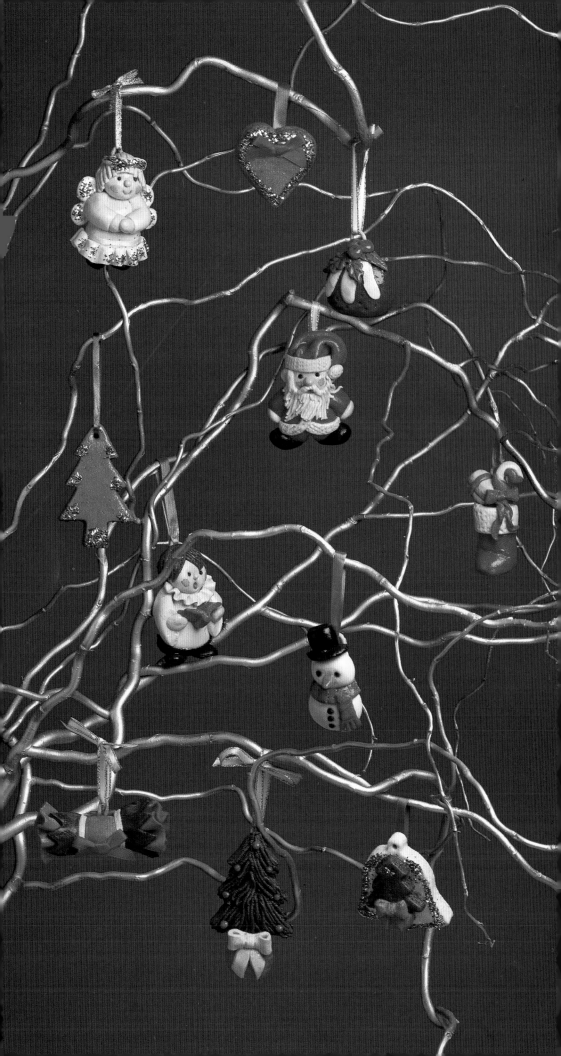

PUPPY IN A KENNEL

You will have no trouble at all finding a good home for this Springer Spaniel puppy. Animal lovers can make the puppy to look just like their own dog, or delight a friend by making the puppy resemble their special pet.

The face is the hardest part of making a dog, and so this project will help you to get the basics right. Any breed of dog will look good in the kennel, or on a cushion or in a basket. Once you have made one puppy, try other breeds.

You will need:
◆ **The basic utensils listed on page 6**
◆ **A quantity of basic dough**

To make the kennel:

1. Roll out a piece of dough to 1cm (½ in) thickness.
2. Cut out a shape 8cm x 10cm (3¼ in x 4in). Trim off each corner at the top.
3. Fix a hanging loop to the centre back of kennel in the same way as for the Alphabet Bear on page 20.
4. For the roof tiles, cut the dough into strips of ½ cm (¼ in) thickness. The tiles measure 2cm (1in) square.
5. Place the first tile at the bottom of the roof and work your way up.
6. Roll out a small sausage for the ridge tile which will join both sides of the roof together.
7. With the back of a knife, mark the kennel with timber panels.

To make the puppy:

1. Roll out two small sausage shapes for the paws and place into position. Make paw marks with tool or knife.
2. For the head, roll dough into a pear shape in the same way as for the Teddy Bear (page 26). A spaniel's head is quite narrow, so shape the head by pressing on each side of the nose. Push the nose up very slightly.
3. Position the head so that the nose is just touching the paws.
4. Using the end of a paintbrush, make a hole at the tip for the nose. Fix a small ball of dough into the hole.

To make the eyes:

1. Because the head of this puppy is long and narrow, the eyes will be positioned more to the side of the face than to the front.
2. Take a small round of dough and squeeze together between the fingers until it is quite thin. Place one on either side of the head.
3. Add a very small black spot.

To make the mouth:

1. Push the end of a paintbrush under the nose to make a hole for the mouth and press slightly downwards to open.
2. Roll small oval shape with points at each end for the tongue. Place one end into the mouth and mark with a knife.

To make the ears:

1. The ears on this puppy are quite large and a very prominent feature.
2. You will need two shapes which resemble leaves. Take a round of dough and roll it into a pear shape, then flatten it between your fingers. One end will be rounded and the other will have a point.
3. Place the pointed end just above the eye and fix.
4. Using a garlic press, make some curls.

To finish:

1. For the dog's bowl, roll a thick sausage and cut a 2cm (¾ in) thick slice. Top up with small off-cuts of dough for biscuits. Place the bowl next to the dog.
2. Make a thin layer of grass around the kennel using the garlic press.

CHEF ON A ROLLING PIN

This cheeky little character is a decorative addition to any kitchen and makes a wonderful gift for a keen cook.

The dough is modelled directly onto the wooden rolling pin. Transfer the completed model and rolling pin together into the oven, you will find that the dough bakes very firmly onto the unvarnished wood.

You will need:
- ◆ The basic utensils listed on page 6
- ◆ A quantity of basic dough
- ◆ 15cm (6in) child's wooden rolling pin
- ◆ String

To make the body, legs & arms:
1. Make a nice smooth egg shape for the body and fix it firmly to the rolling pin. Do this just as you would fix dough pieces together, by wetting the surfaces with a paint brush.
2. Attach a hanging loop to the back of the chef (follow the directions given with the Alphabet Bear on page 20).
3. Make sausage shapes for the legs and fix to the body and rolling pin.
4. For the shoes, form two small balls of dough into a smooth pear shape, Attach to the legs and turn each shoe out slightly. When it looks right, also attach each one to the rolling pin.
5. For the arms, roll out a piece of dough to approximately 1cm (½ in) thickness. Cut two lengths, cut the top of each length in a slant to fit the arm to the shoulder.
6. For hands, attach small rounds of dough to the end of each arm and secure to the legs.

7. For the jacket, make small dents for the buttons, and fill each one in with a small round of dough.

To make the head:
1. Roll a round of dough for the head, try it against the body to check that it is in proportion, and fix it to the body.
2. With the end of your paintbrush, push a small hole for the nose in the centre of the face. Fill with a little ball of dough.
3. Make two holes for the eyes, give the chef a big smile with the curved-ended tool.
4. For the ears, fix two small rounds of dough to the sides of the head.
5. For the scarf, roll two small pieces of dough into oblong shapes and squeeze each one gently between your fingers to shape it, these will make the ends of the neckerchief. Place them under the chin, and add small round of dough for the knot.

6. For the chef's sideboards, roll out a small strip of dough very thinly. Cut two small oblongs and place each one in front of an ear. Mark them with a knife blade to give the effect of hair.

7. For the moustache, roll a very small amount of dough between your fingers and place it under the nose. Turn up the ends for a comical effect.

Chef's hat

Making the chef's hat is the trickiest part of the operation. You may want to practise it first. Roll a round of spare dough into a practice 'head' and follow the instructions.

To make the hat:

1. Roll out a piece of dough to about ¾ cm (⅜ in) thickness and cut out a circle 10cm (4in) in diameter.

2. Wet the edges of the circle, place it on top of the head and gather it all around the edges. Use the end of a paintbrush or a cocktail stick to help push the dough into place.

3. Work from the middle of the forehead around to each side.

4. Now shape the hat with your fingers, squeezing the edges and elongating the hat so that it is tall and narrower at the bottom.

5. For the hat band, cut a thin strip of dough, place the band across the head, keeping it quite tight. Trim off the excess.

6. The hat should now be in place, well above the chef's eyes. With a fingertip on top of the hat, push it downwards and a little to one side to give the chef character - again, this may take a little practice to get the effect just right.

Loaf of bread

Bread is easy and fun to make. Position the finished loaves as shown in the photograph.

THATCHED COTTAGE

This little thatched cottage makes a charming ornament for any country lover, but it is a real test of your skills. Visitors are sure to admire it - you could find yourself taking orders for more!

You will need a ruler to help you to line things up more easily and take a few measurements.

You will need:
- The basic utensils listed on page 6
- A quantity of basic dough
- Ruler
- String

To make the cottage:
1. Roll out a piece of dough to ½ cm (¼ in) thickness. Cut out a piece measuring 7cm x 8½cm (2¾ in x 3½in). This is the base for the cottage.
2. Cut off the corners diagonally at each side to form the roof slope.
3. Secure a hanging loop firmly to the back (follow the directions given with the Alphabet Bear on page 20).

To make the windows:
1. With your fingers, shape a ball of dough into a cube 1½ cm (¾ in) square and ½ cm (¼ in) thick.
2. Make two of these for the upstairs windows and place them 1½ cm (¾ in) below the top of the roof.
3. For the downstairs windows cut two squares measuring 1¼ cm (½ in) and ¼ cm (⅛ in) thick. Place these to line up with the top of the door.
4. Cut small strips for the window ledges and place beneath each window.

5. For the window panes, roll out a small piece of dough very thinly and cut a thin strip. Chop the strip into small squares and place them neatly on the windows.

To make the door:
1. Roll a piece of dough ½ cm (¼ in) thick and cut out a rectangle 1½cm x 1cm (¾ in x ½ in) Mark panels on the door with a tool or knife.

2. Place the door between the two lower windows. Add tiny pieces of dough for hinges and a door knob. Put a small step under the door.

3. Arrange two small oblong pieces together to form a porch.

To make the thatched roof:

1. Press dough out through the garlic press and begin layering thatch onto the roof from halfway down the upstairs windows, starting at one end and working in a line to the far end.

2. Make the second and third layers slightly longer, so that the third layer reaches the top of the roof.
3. Cover the sides of the roof.
4. For the pattern across the roof, lay out a single strand of dough from the garlic press the width of the cottage.
5. With a circular cutter or a plastic pen top, make half-circles all the way along the dough.
6. Lift the strip carefully with the tip of a knife blade and place it along the top of the roof.
7. Using the end of your paintbrush, push two holes into the dough to take the chimneys.
8. Roll two small balls of dough for the chimneys, push them into the holes and finish off the chimneys with a small round on top of each one.

To finish:

1. Press out some grass with the garlic press and lay around the cottage.
2. Add some flowers to bring colour to the garden.

BOWL OF FRUIT AND FLOWERS

If you have worked through most of the projects so far, you will really be developing a feel for doughcraft by now and this project should be well within your capabilities. It is quite a challenge and calls for quite delicate modelling.

I have chosen to paint this project, rather than using coloured dough, because the paints can be used to add further depths of light and shade to the model. As you paint, be aware of the direction the light is coming from, and darken or lighten tones accordingly. If you find you have made a colour too light or too dark, don't worry, just go over it again when the paint has dried.

You will need:
◆ The basic utensils listed on page 6
◆ A quantity of basic dough
◆ String
◆ Cloves

To make the bowl

1. Cut out or trace the template from the back of the Workstation.
2. Roll out the dough to a thickness of 1½ cm (¾ in). Using a sharp knife, cut around the template and place the dough onto the baking sheet.
3. Gently soften the edges of the bowl with your fingers to give a more rounded appearance and prick all over with a fork or cocktail stick.
4. Mark the foot of the bowl with the back of a knife and twist a small strip for the rope-effect trimming.
5. Make the hanging loop by cutting a strip of dough 1½ cm x 7cm (¾ in x 3in). Moisten the ends of a short length of string and fix it to the bowl with the strip of dough. This needs to be well done as the loop will support the weight of the finished model.

To make the leaves:

1. Roll out dough to ¼ cm (⅛ in) thick and cut out six leaves.
2. For the apples, make one large round shape and two smaller ones.
3. Make two pear shapes.
4. Assemble the fruit and leaves onto the bowl. Remember to wet the bowl *and* the fruit, and fix them firmly.
5. Roll out small rounds of dough to make the grapes and arrange them, use the photograph as a guide.

To make the flowers:

1. Make five small rounds of dough and press each one into a pear shape, pinching one end together.
2. Roll a small round for the flower centre and arrange the five petals around it. Prick the centre with a cocktail stick to give it texture. You need two flowers made the same way.
3. For the rosebuds, flatten a small length of dough between your fingers and roll the dough inwards, from left to right. When the bud is large enough, twist the dough to break off the excess. You will need two rosebuds.

Painting the model

You can have great fun exploring shades of light and dark when painting this piece. Paint the bowl first. Use a slightly darker shade for the first coat. Leave it to dry then apply a slightly lighter shade for a second coat. Work very slightly darker shades under the leaves to add depth. In the same way, paint the leaves and fruit with a slightly darker first coat, leave to dry. Apply second and subsequent coats in a lighter shade, working carefully until you have the most realistic effect.

The bloom on the grapes is achieved by painting a lighter shade on top of a darker one.

VICTORIAN GIRL

Little girls will be delighted by this pretty character. You can make her look quite different by changing her hair style, hat or dress. The basic body shape is also easy to dress up in boy's clothes to make a pair.

You will need:
◆ The basic utensils listed on page 6
◆ A quantity of basic dough

To make the legs and body:
1. Roll out with your fingers a length of dough approximately 16cm (6½ in) long and 1cm (½ in) thick. The length of the legs will determine the size of the doll.
2. Fold the dough in half, shoes will be attached to the loose ends.
3. For the body, make an egg shape and fix it to the top of the legs.
4. Make a hanging loop, following the directions given for the Alphabet Bear on page 20. Attach it to the back of the body.

To make the shoes:
1. Roll out two pear shapes to the appropriate size, pressing down the top slightly.
2. Place a small thin round on the top of each shoe, leaving about one-third uncovered at the front.
3. Fix the shoes to the ends of the legs, being careful not to push the legs out of shape.
4. Make a thin strap to go around each ankle and fix to the shoes. Add a tiny round button.

To make the petticoat:
1. Roll out a piece of dough to ¼ cm (⅛ in) thickness and cut a strip 16cm (6½ in) long and 2.5cm (1in) wide.
2. Frill the strip like a concertina, passing the dough between your fingers. Lay the frill down on the worktop and press your finger down one edge to secure the frills.
3. Use a pizza wheel or a knife to trim.
4. Place the frill just above the ankles.

To make the skirt:
1. Roll dough out to ¼ cm (⅛ in) thickness and cut a length measuring approximately 4cm x 20cm (1¾ in x 8in). Check the size against the legs

and trim if necessary.

2. Make a frill in the same way as for the petticoat, and fix it to the lower edge of the skirt. Check for length.

3. Make three folds in the skirt and lay it across the body, leaving the petticoat showing.

4. Arrange the folds so that they 'fall' in an attractive way. This may need some practice before it looks just as it should.

5. Hold the skirt against the body. If the top comes above the waistline, trim it before fixing. Fix the skirt to the body.

6. Cut a wide band to cover the join at the waist. Using the serrated-edge tool, trim it with 'stitching'.

To make the collar:

1. Cut out two round shapes, approximately 2½ cm (1in) in diameter and trim one-third off each.

2. Place the two parts of the collar so that they meet in the middle of the body and cover the joins at the arms.

3. Decorate with 'stitching' marks.

To make the head:

With this doll, you are aiming for a pretty face, rather than the comical ones of the chef or clown, so you might prefer to practise first on a spare piece of dough. The proportions and spacing need to be right to get the best effect. If the eyes are too close or too far apart, or the mouth too low, the face won't look right.

1. Roll out the head to size. Try it against the body to check the proportions are correct, then fix it to the body.

2. Make a hole for the nose in the centre, and fix a small piece of dough into the hole.

3. Make holes for the eyes using a cocktail stick.

4. Make the mouth using the curved ended tool.

5. For the hair, feed pieces of dough through the garlic press until you have the length required. You will need six strands for each plait.

6. Lay the strands out on the worktop and plait six together to the length required. Squeeze the top to hold it in place. Place each plait on the side of the face, high enough up for the top to be covered by the hat.

7. Add a bow to the end of each plait, fix it to the arm.

To make the hat:

1. Roll and cut out a large circle, about 8cm (3¼ in) in diameter.

2. Trim off one third.

3. Fix the straight side to the back of the head and arrange the brim attractively around the face.

MAISIE'S CREATIONS

As you can see, there is almost no limit to the shapes and characters
you can make from dough. This book will get you started -
the rest is up to you, and your imagination!

ABCD
EFGHI
JKLM
NOPQ
RSTUV
WXYZ

BOOK *and* BOW
for Teddy Bears - page 26

BOOK

BOW

TAILS FOR BOW

TROUSERS
*for Clown - page 28
and Santa - page 32*

BRACES
for Clown

HAT
*for Santa Claus
- page 32*

*LEAVES and BASE
for Candleholders
- page 34*

*CHRISTMAS DECORATIONS
- page 36*

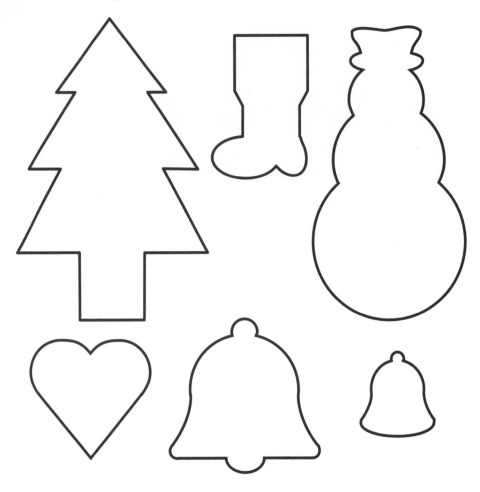

KENNEL, and PUPPY'S EARS - page 38

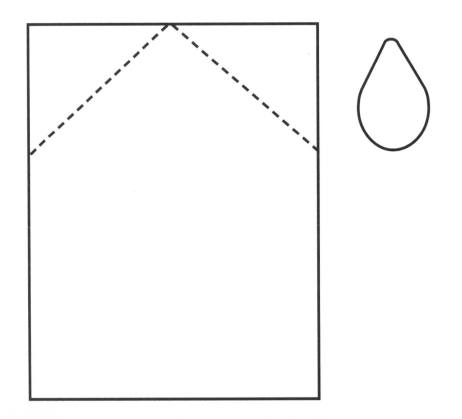

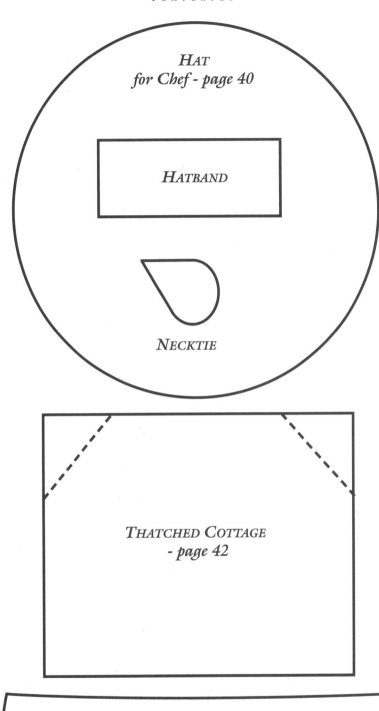

HAT
for Chef - page 40

HATBAND

NECKTIE

THATCHED COTTAGE
- page 42

FRUIT BOWL -
page 44

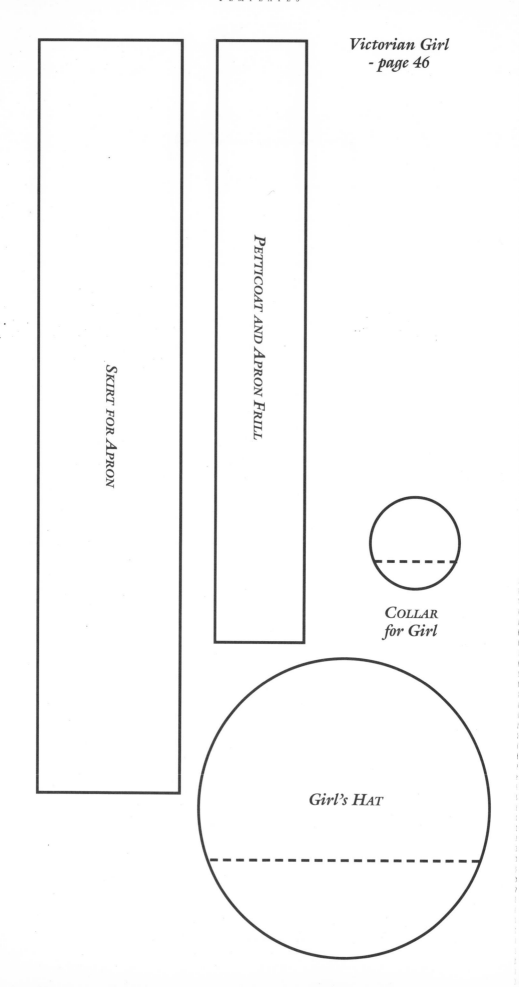

Victorian Girl
- page 46

PETTICOAT AND APRON FRILL

SKIRT FOR APRON

COLLAR
for Girl

Girl's HAT

All templates are full size, unless indicated

GENERAL: *Useful sizes of cutters*

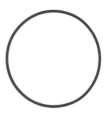

USEFUL SIZES *for petals and leaves*

PETAL SHAPE
for flower brooch
- page 16

HAT *and* WING
for Duck Brooch
- page 18

HAT *and* PLATES
- page 16 and 18

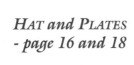

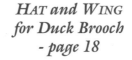

EARS
for Pig Brooch
- page 19

HEART
for Alphabet Bear
- page 20

ALPHABETS
for Alphabet Bear - page 20

Enlarge on a photocopier to the size required.

abcde
fghijkl
mnop
qrstuv
wxyz